Ostereier

Färbung Buch

Coloring Pages for Kids

Coloring Pages for Kids
An imprint of Ciparum LLC

Ostereier Färbung Buch
© 2017 Ciparum LLC
All rights reserved.
ISBN-10:1-63589-480-8
ISBN-13:978-1-63589-480-6

Coloring Pages for Kids

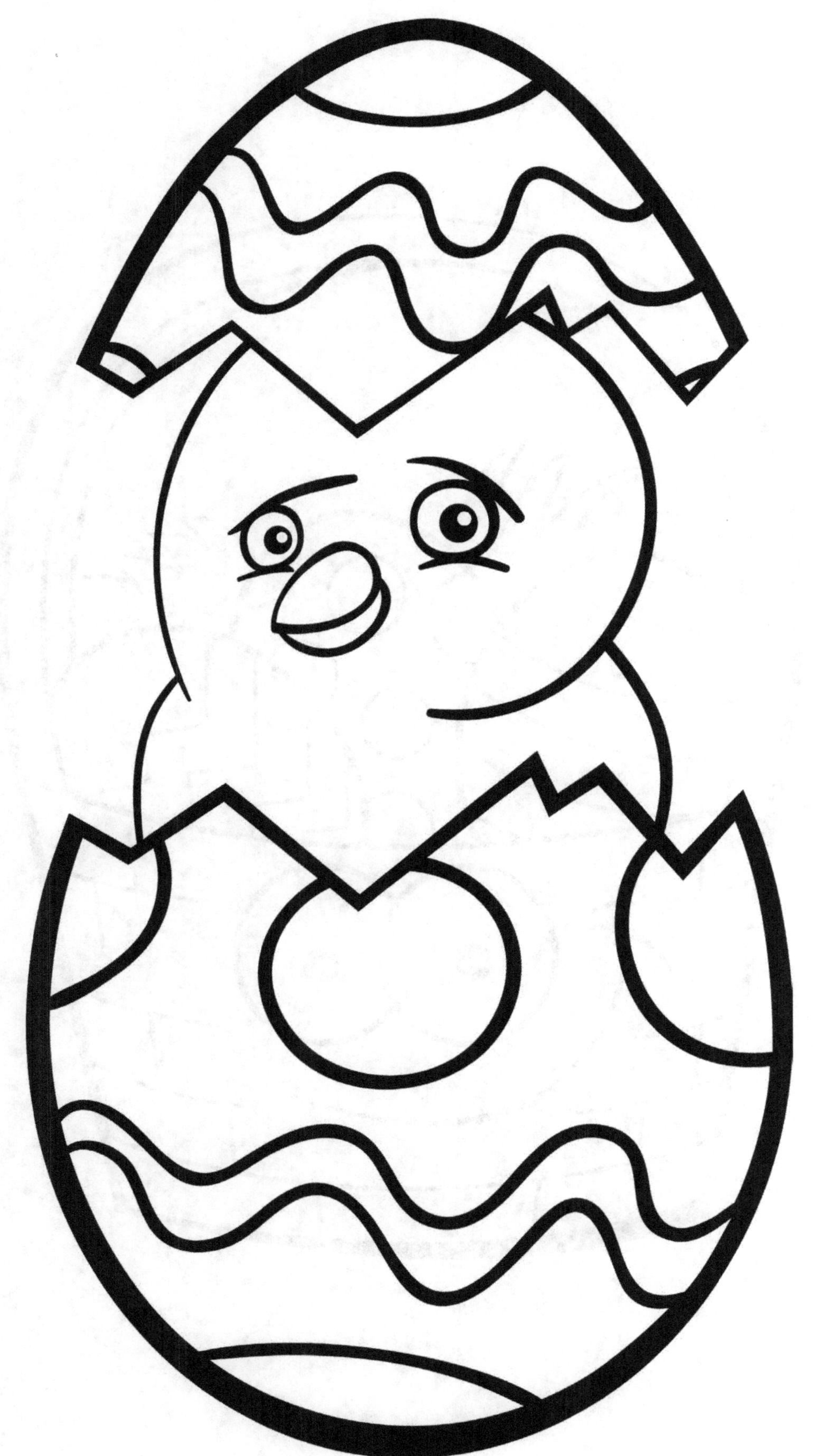

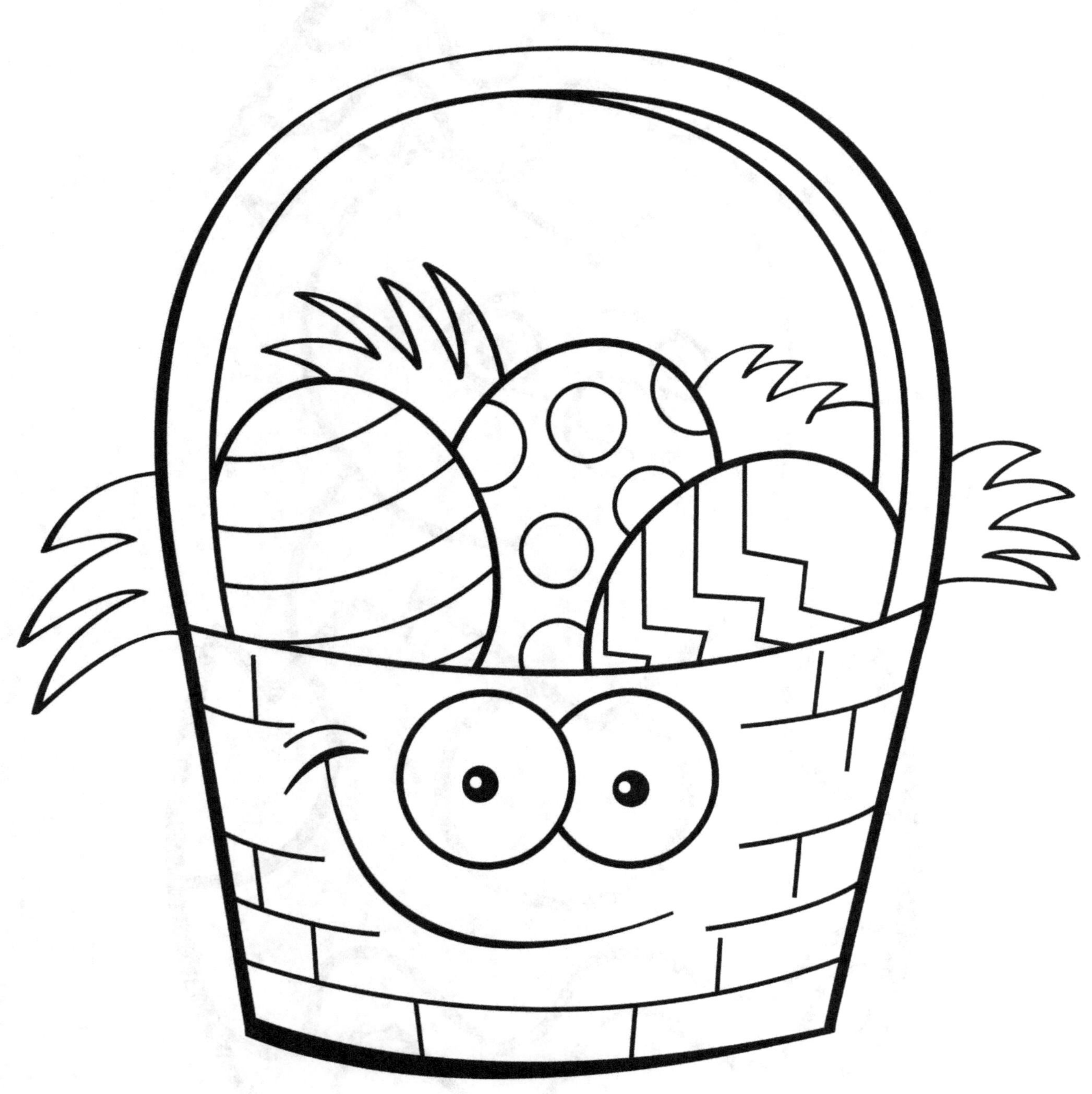

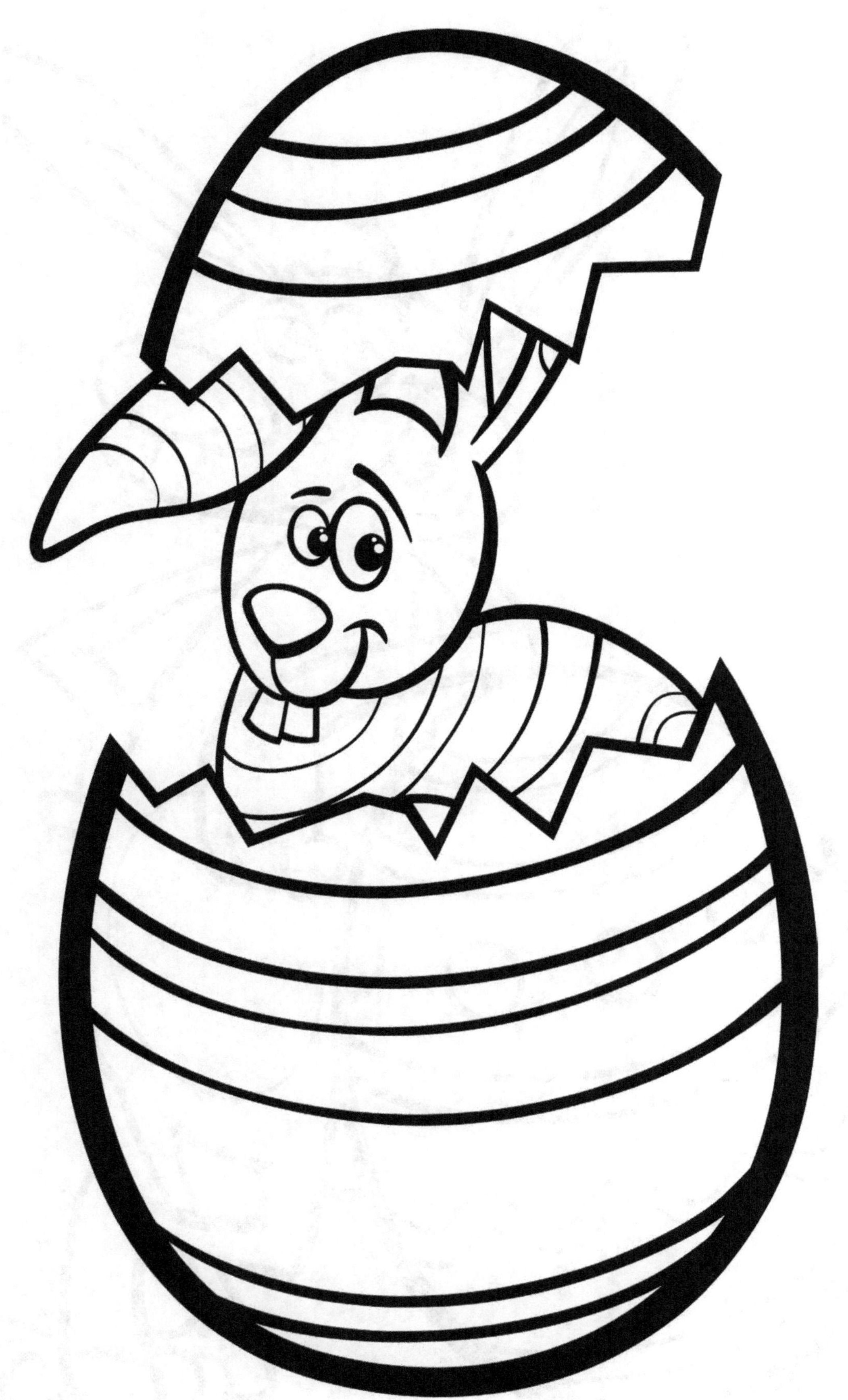

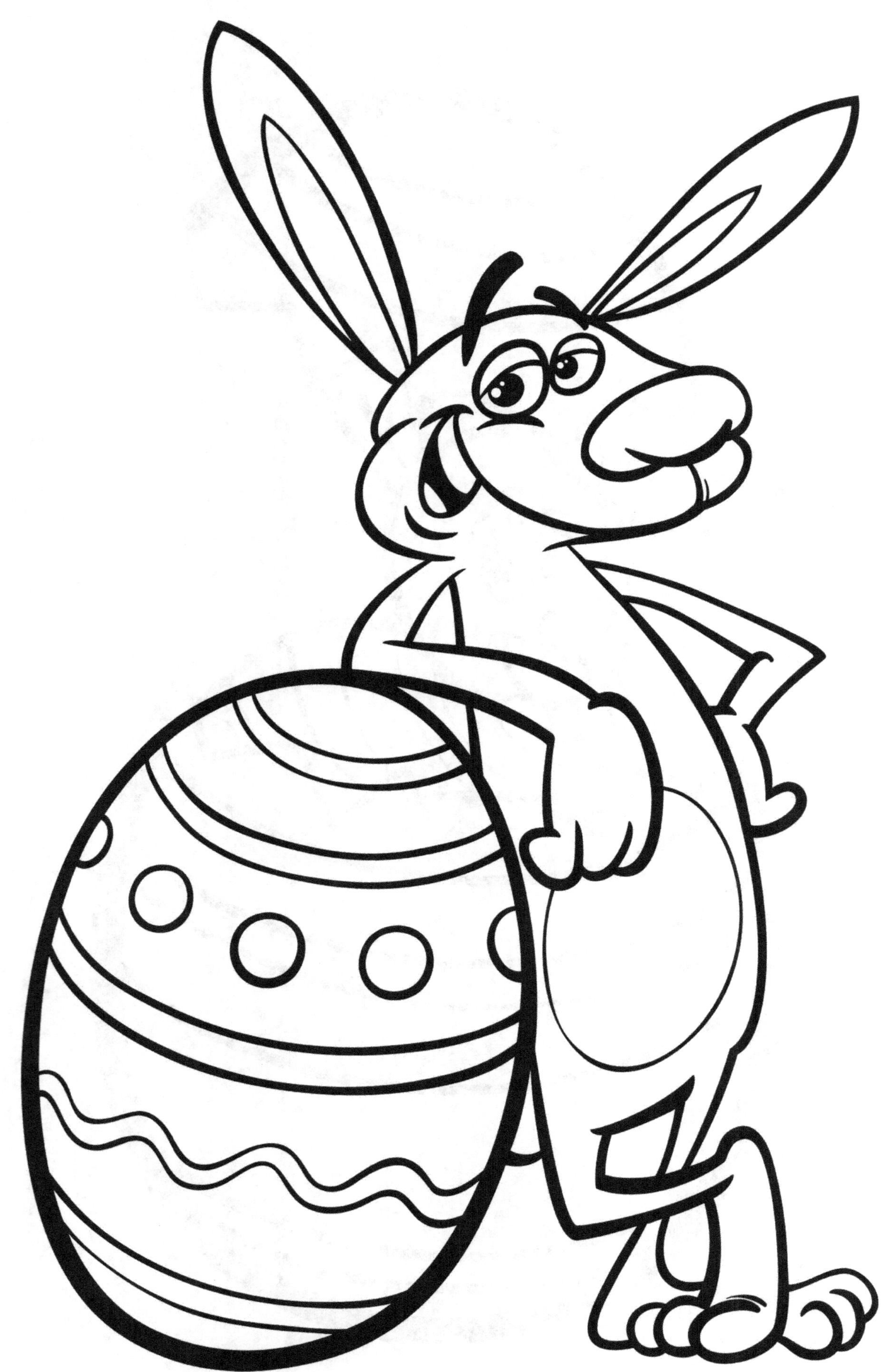

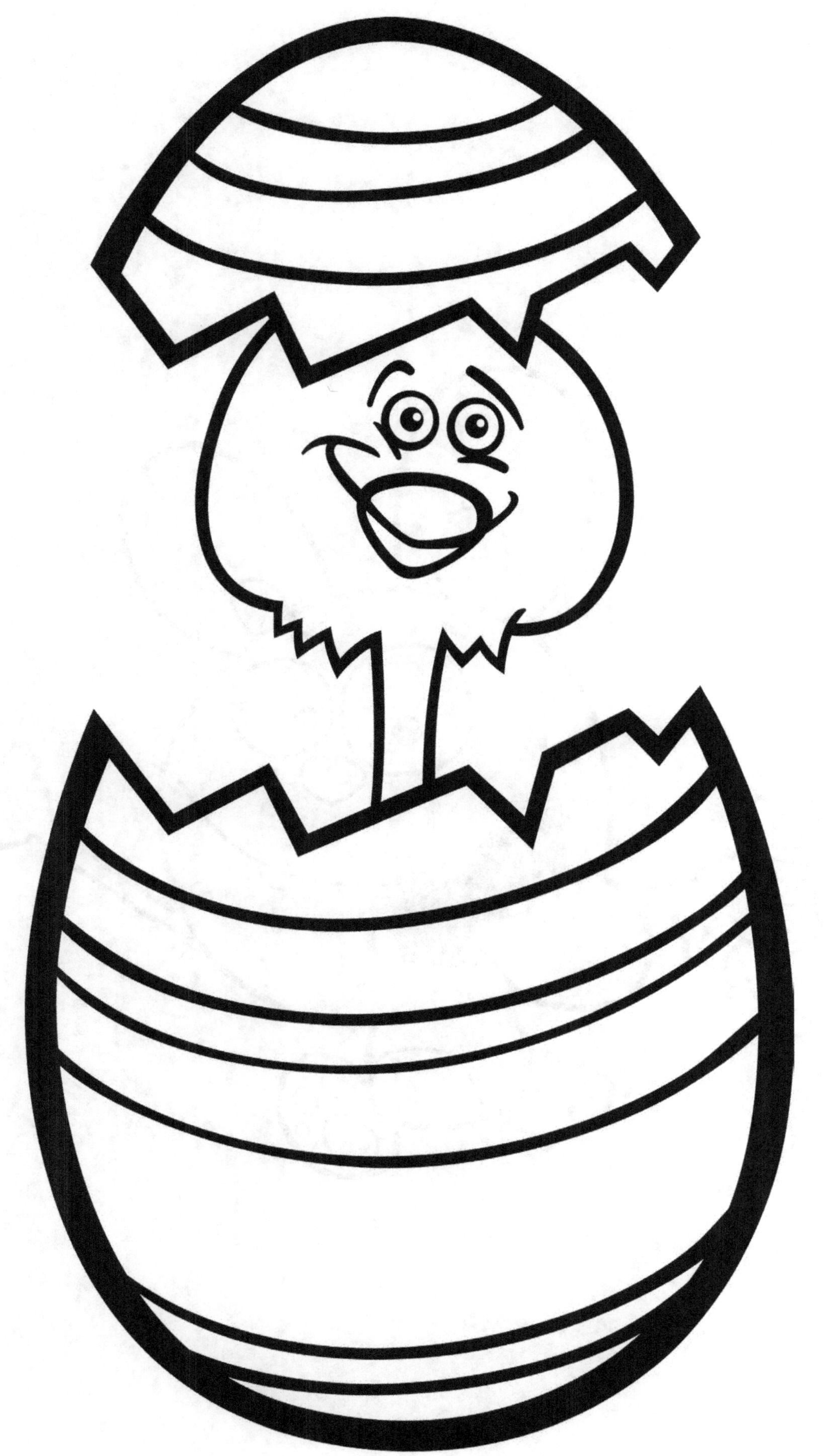

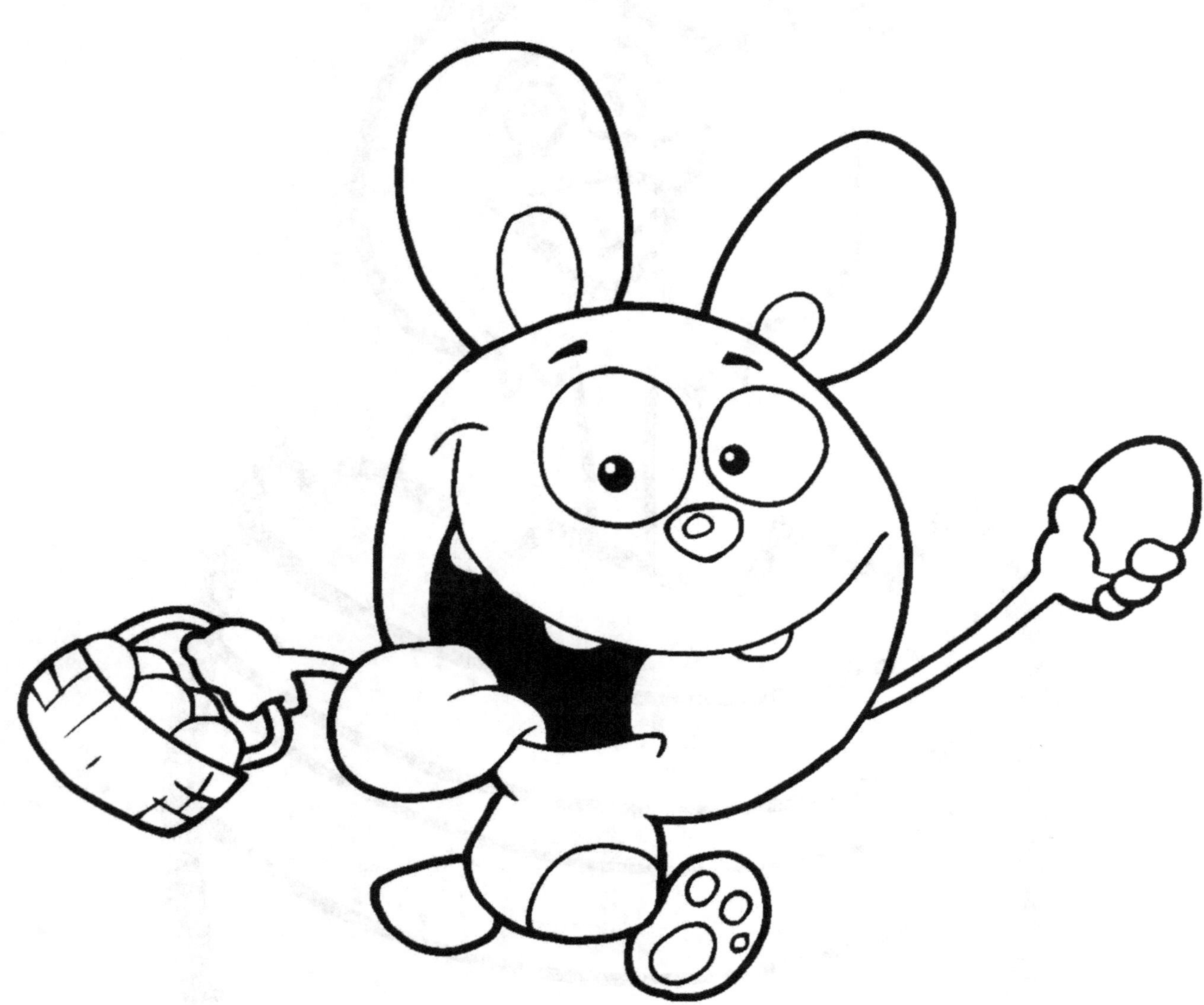

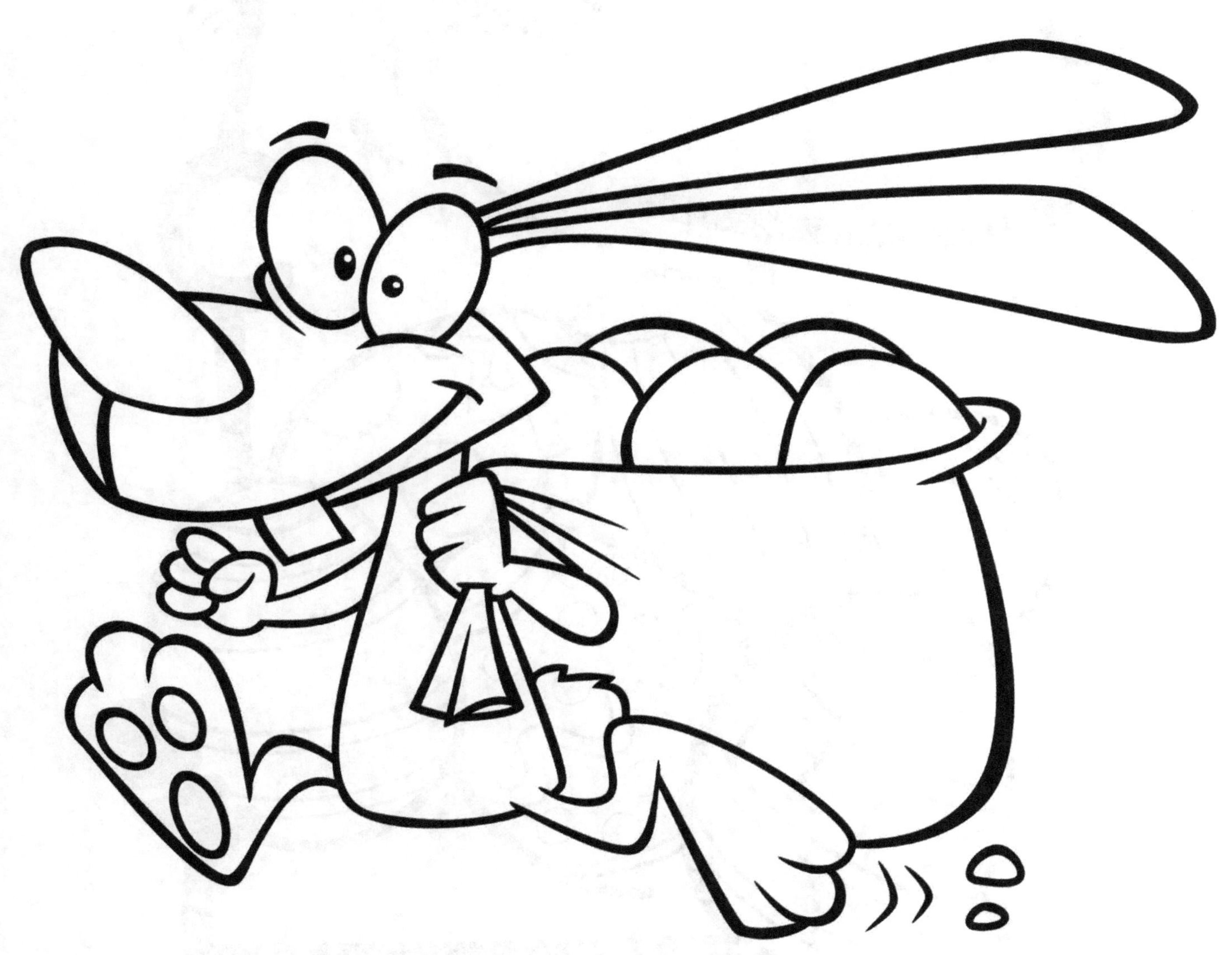

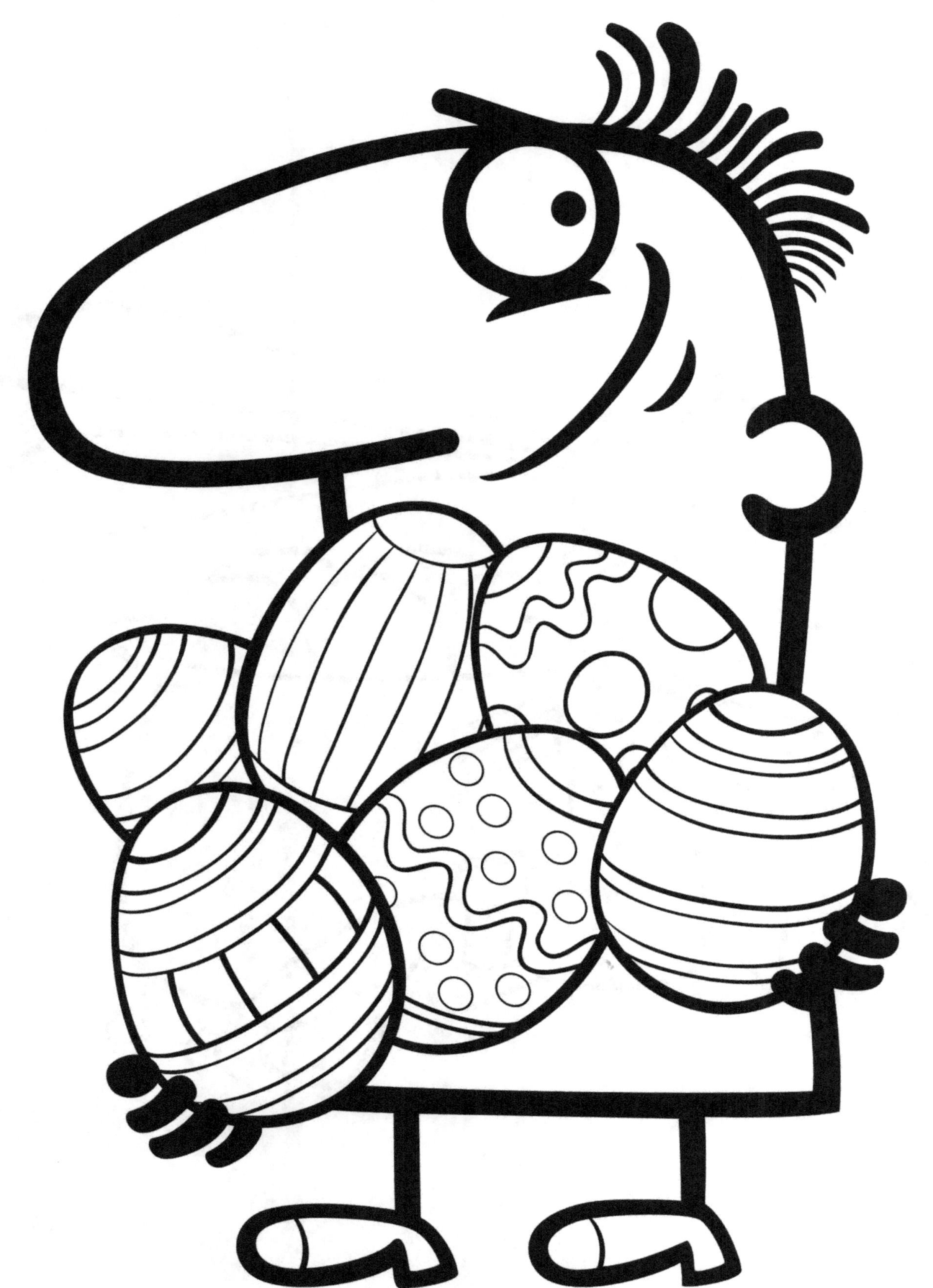

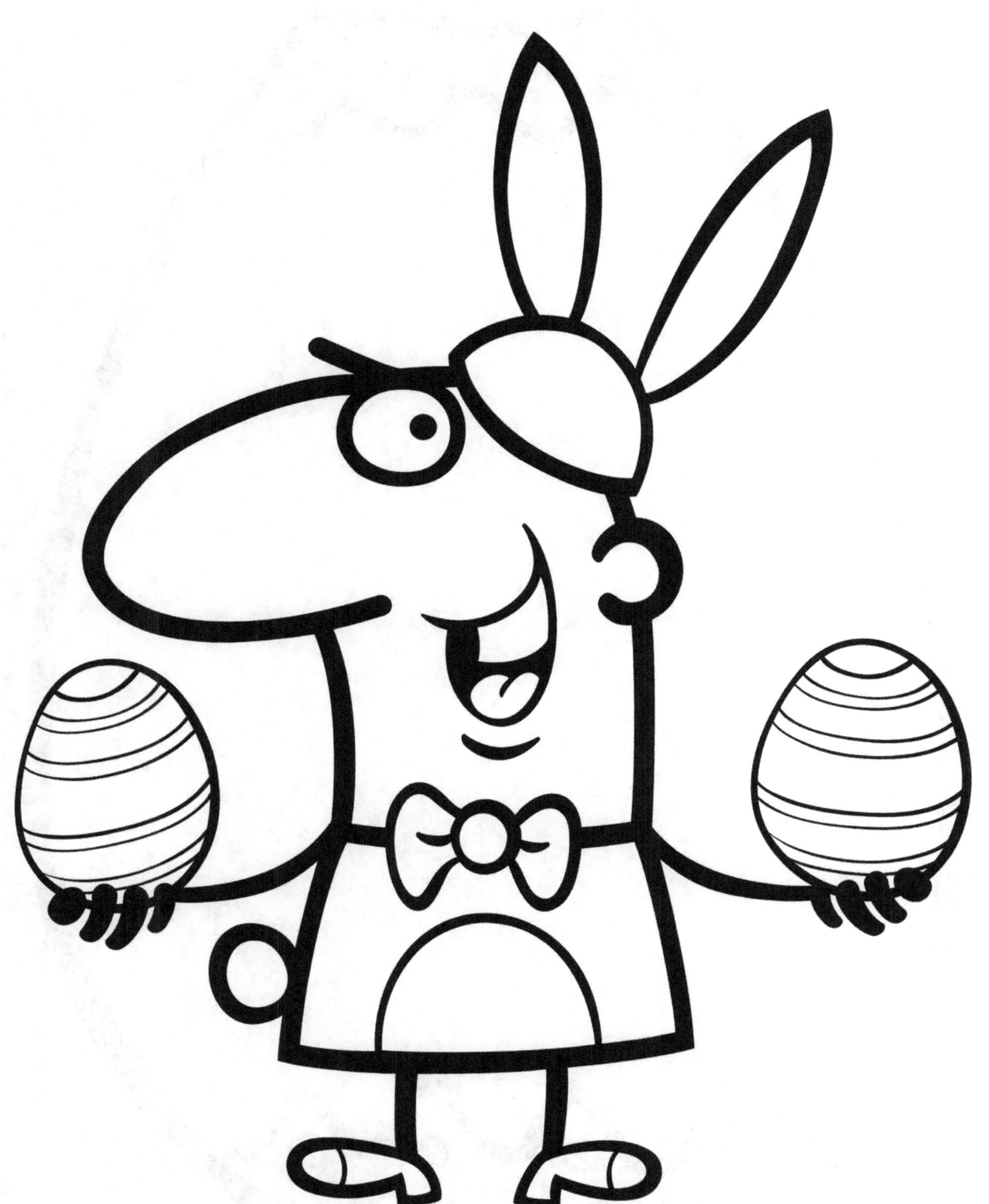

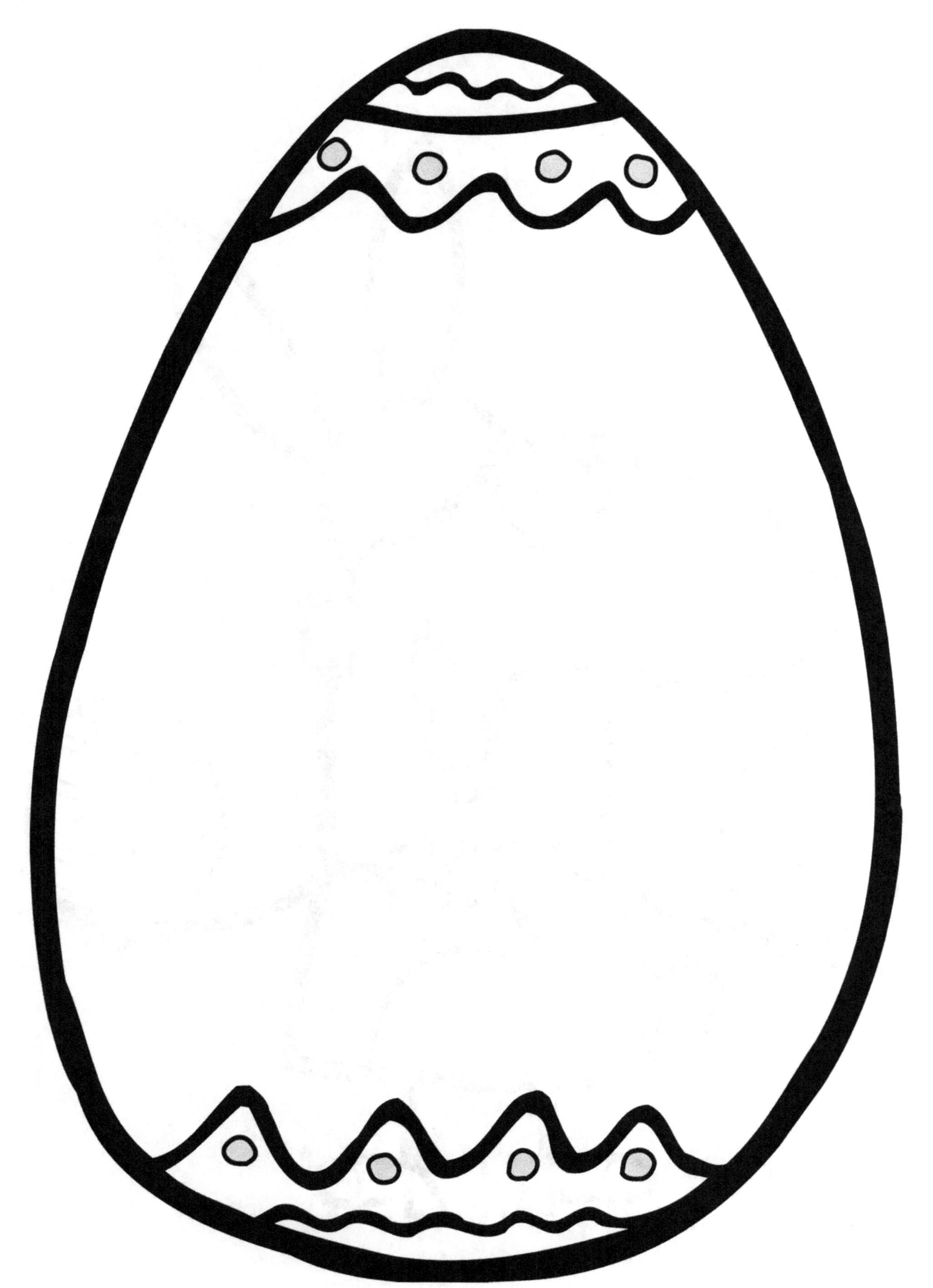

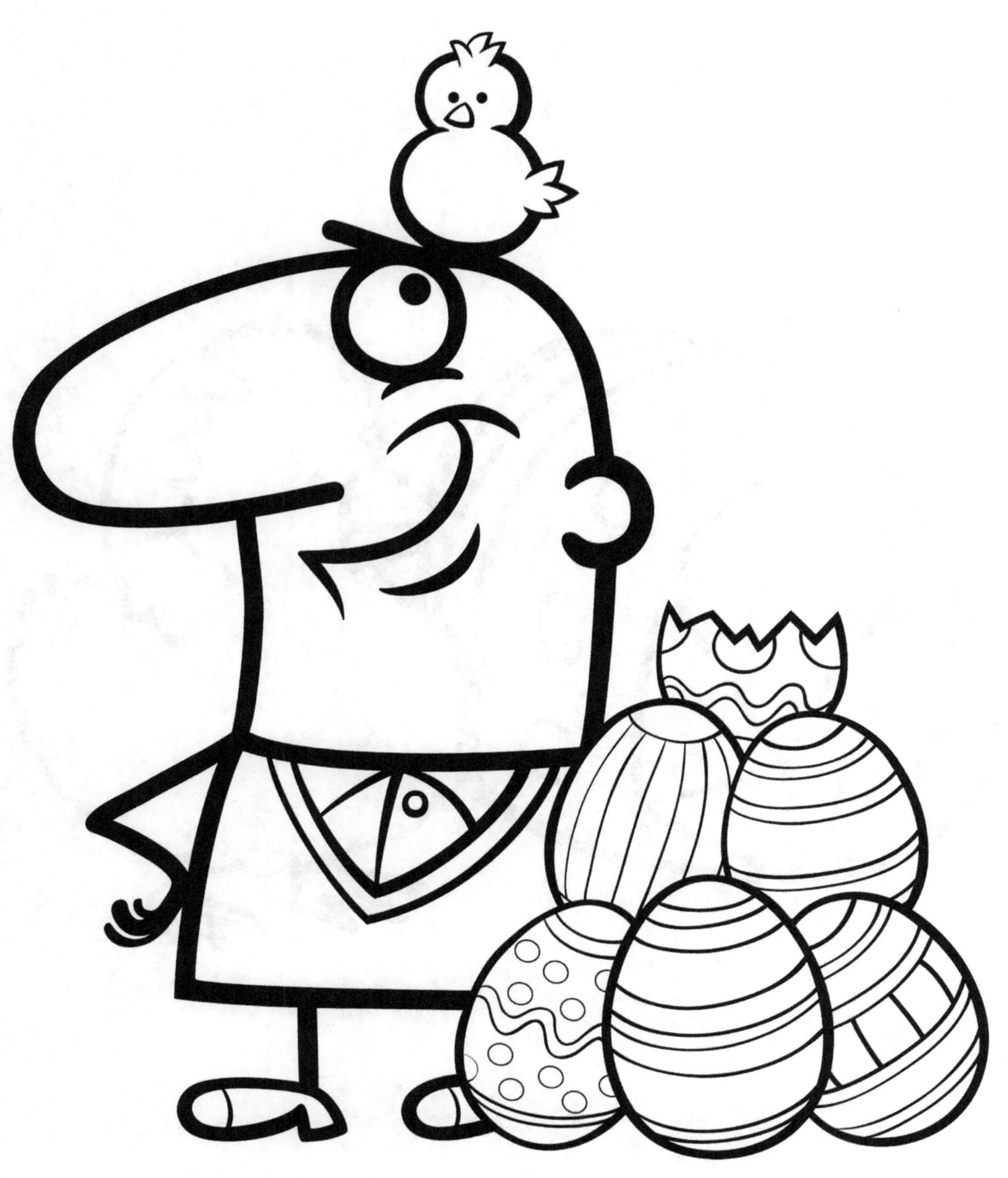

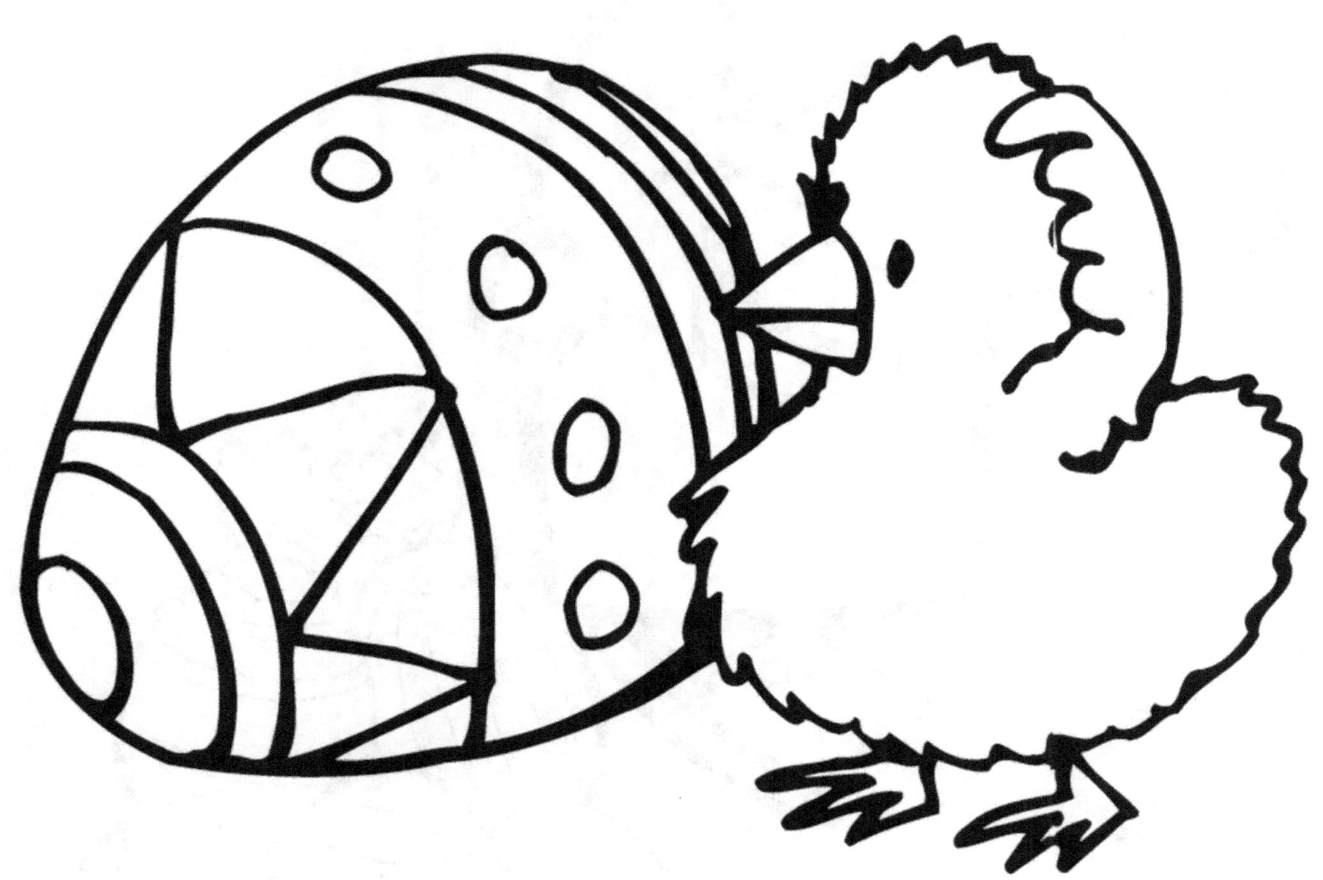

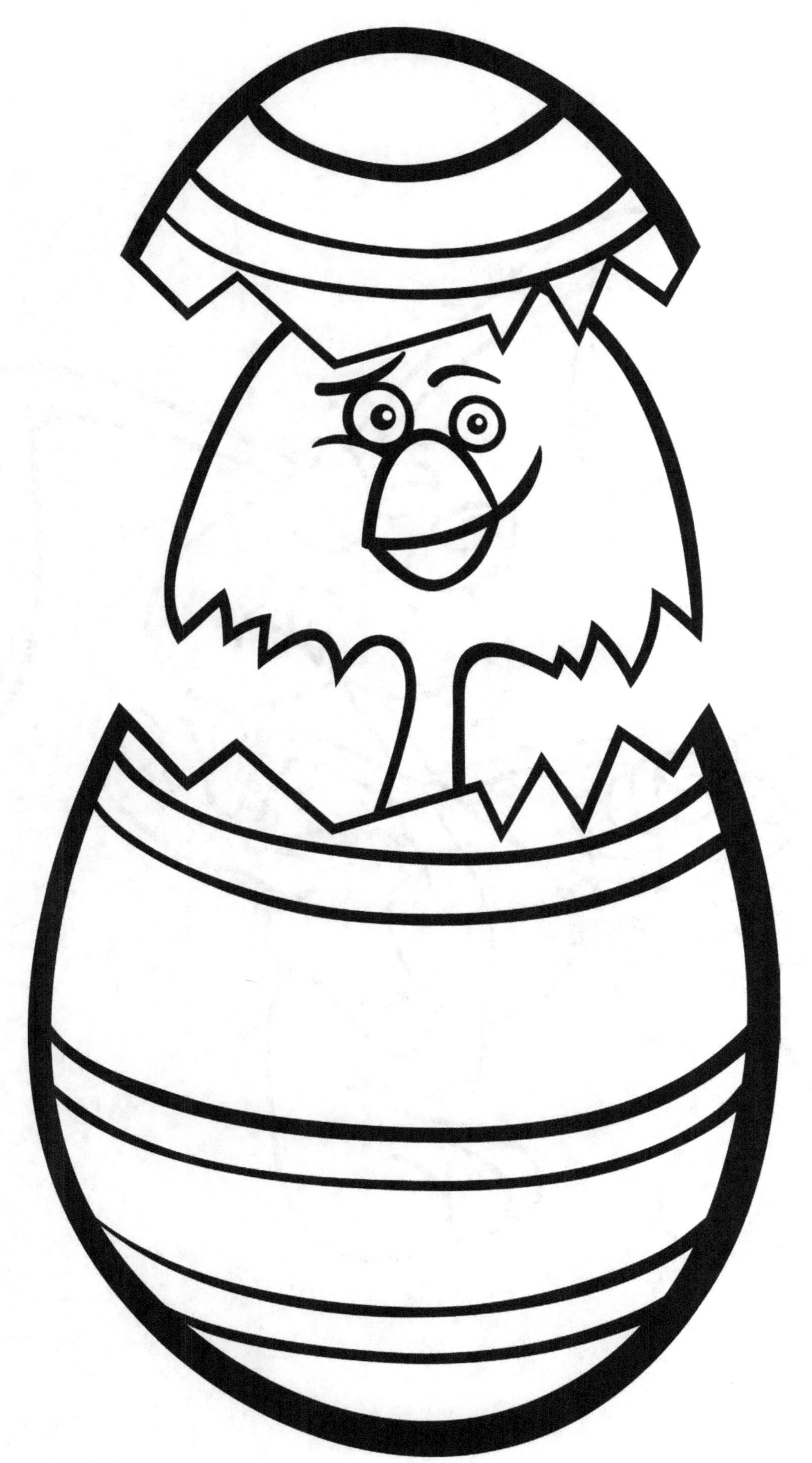

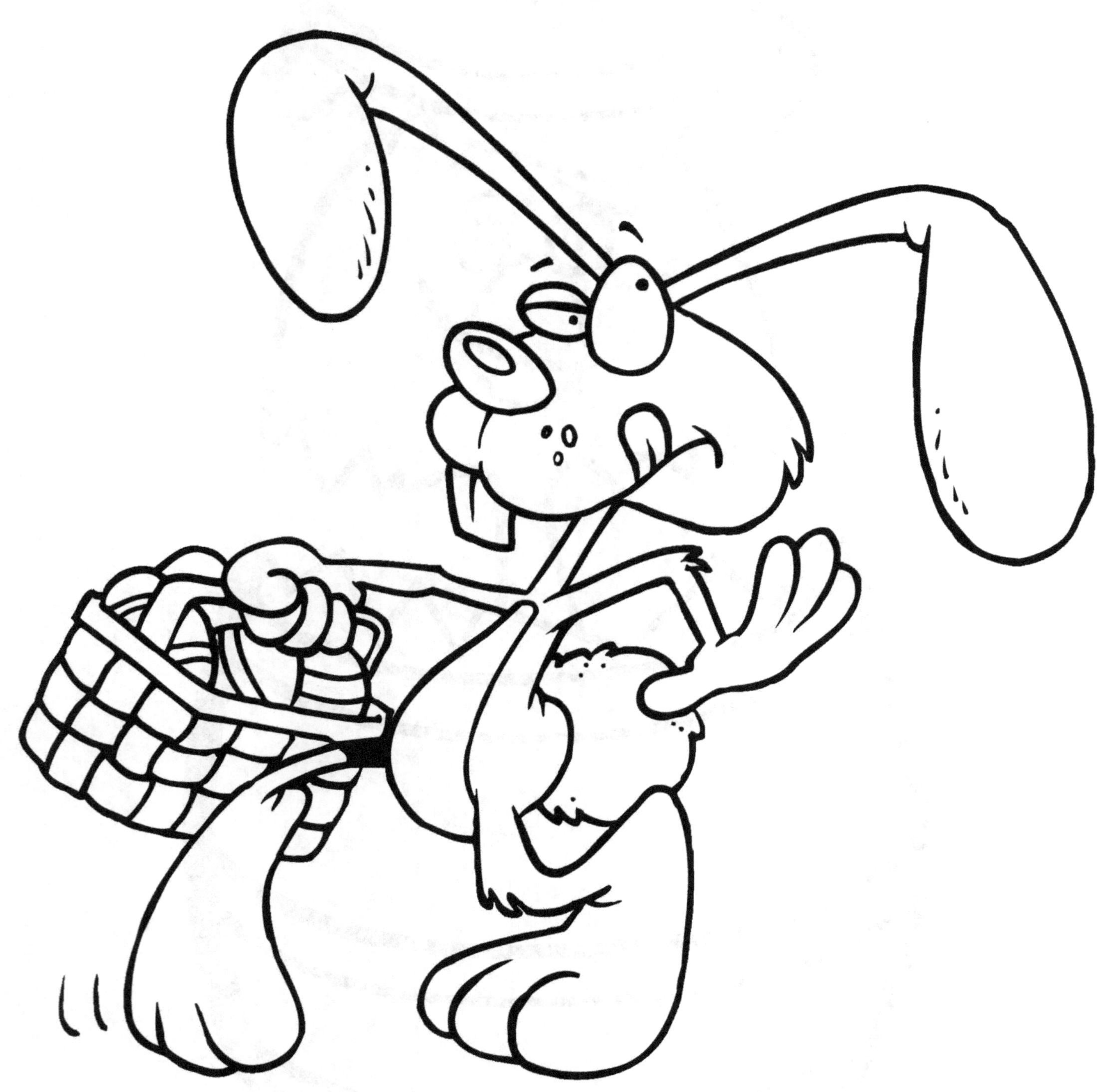

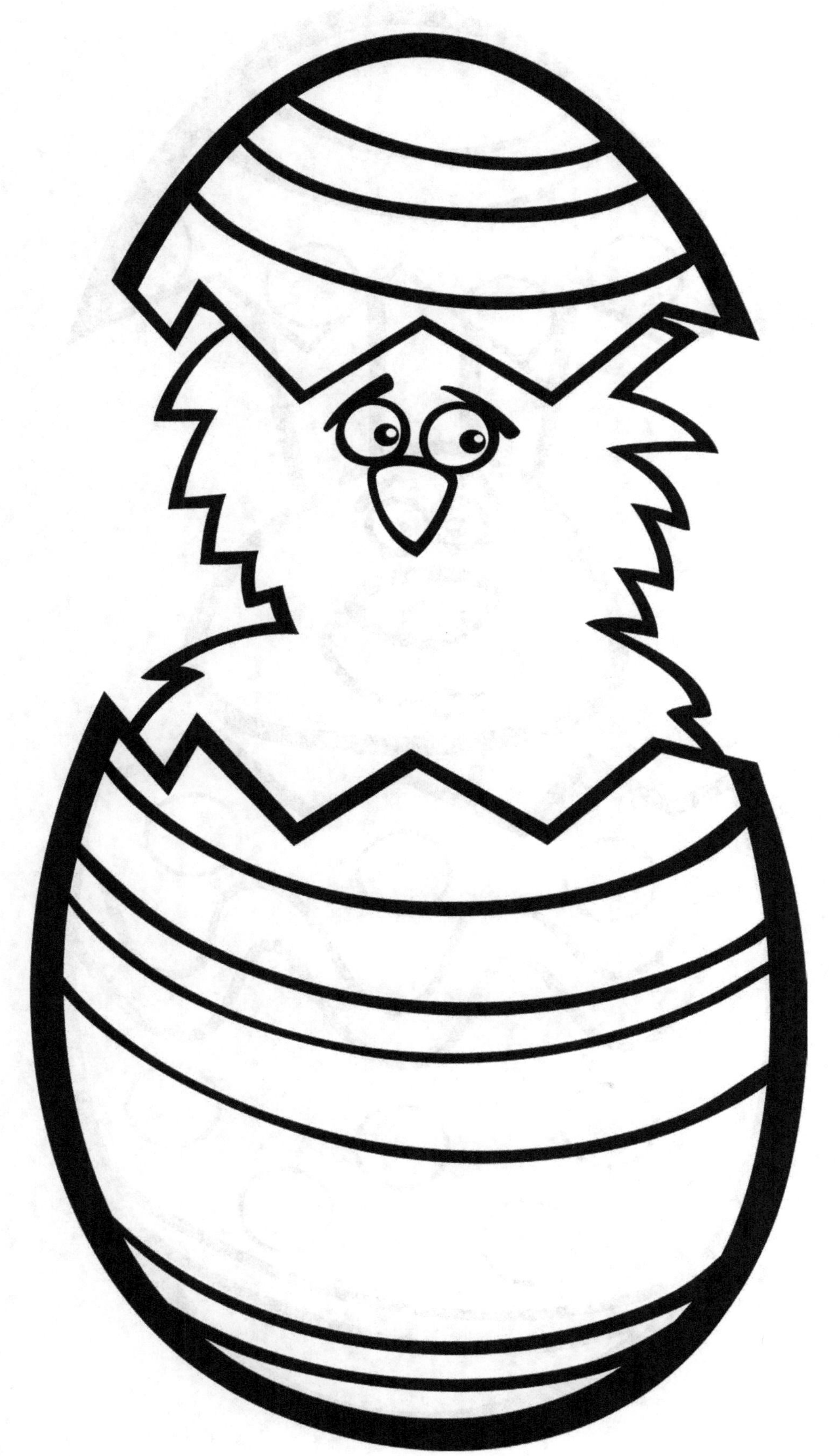

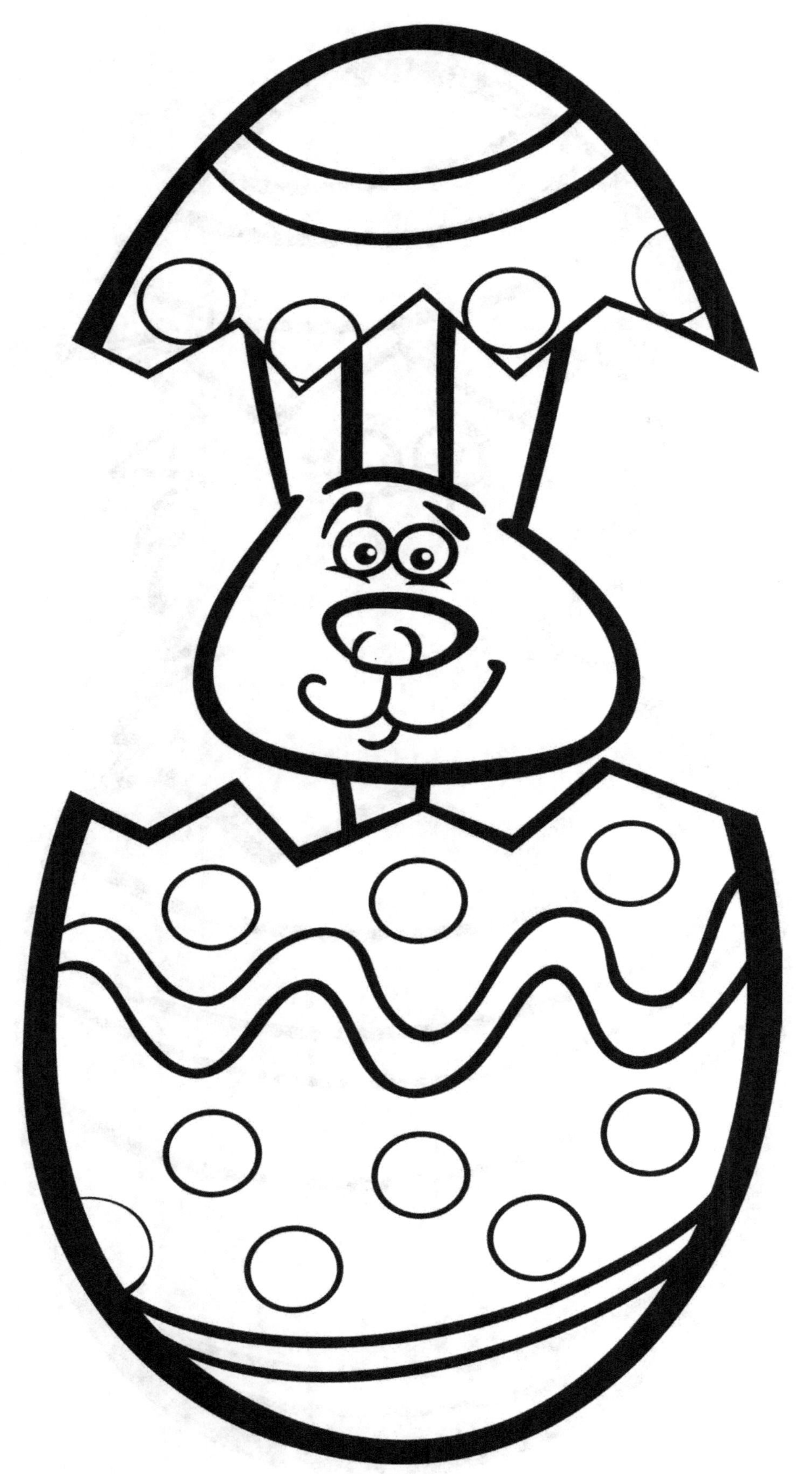

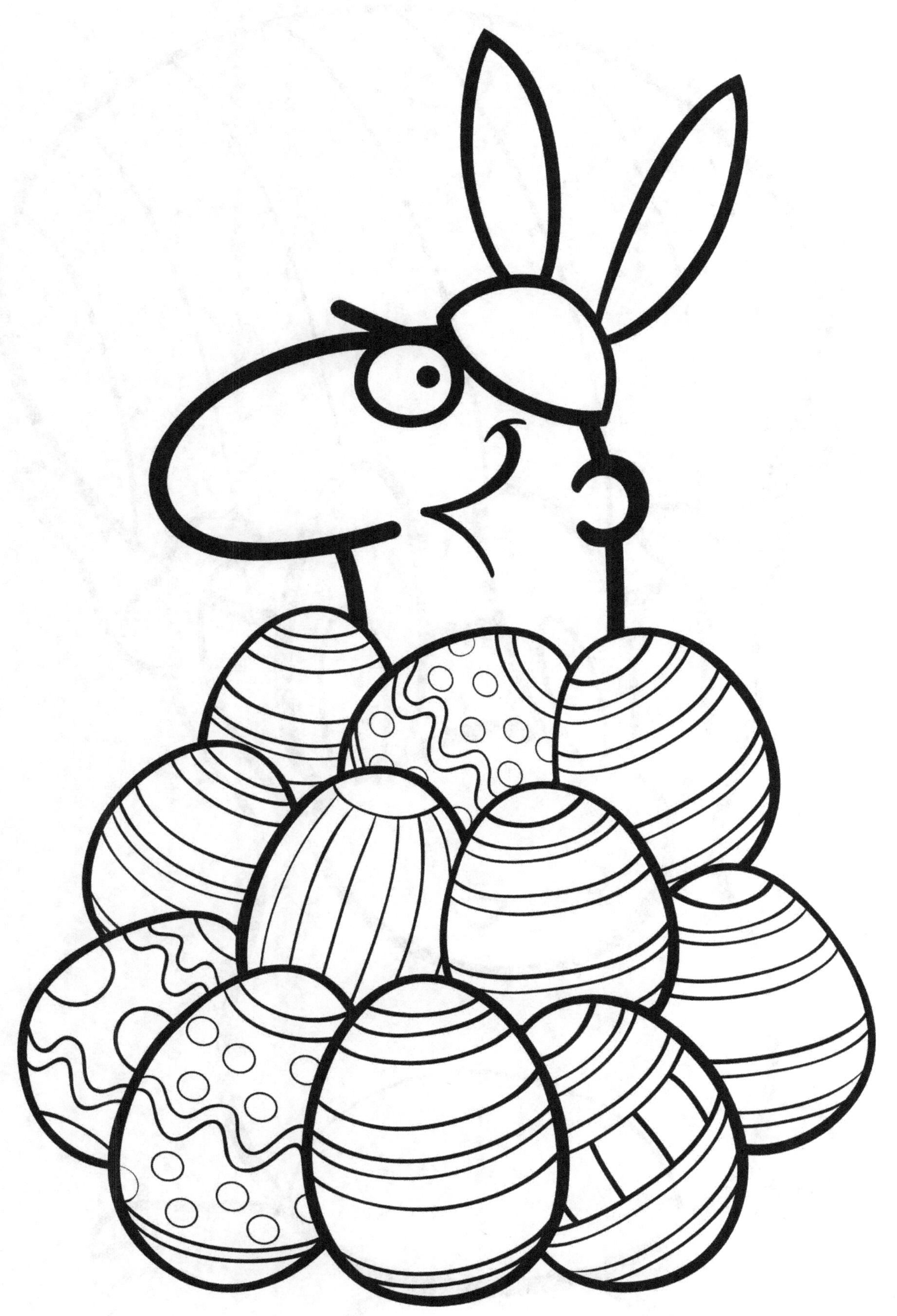

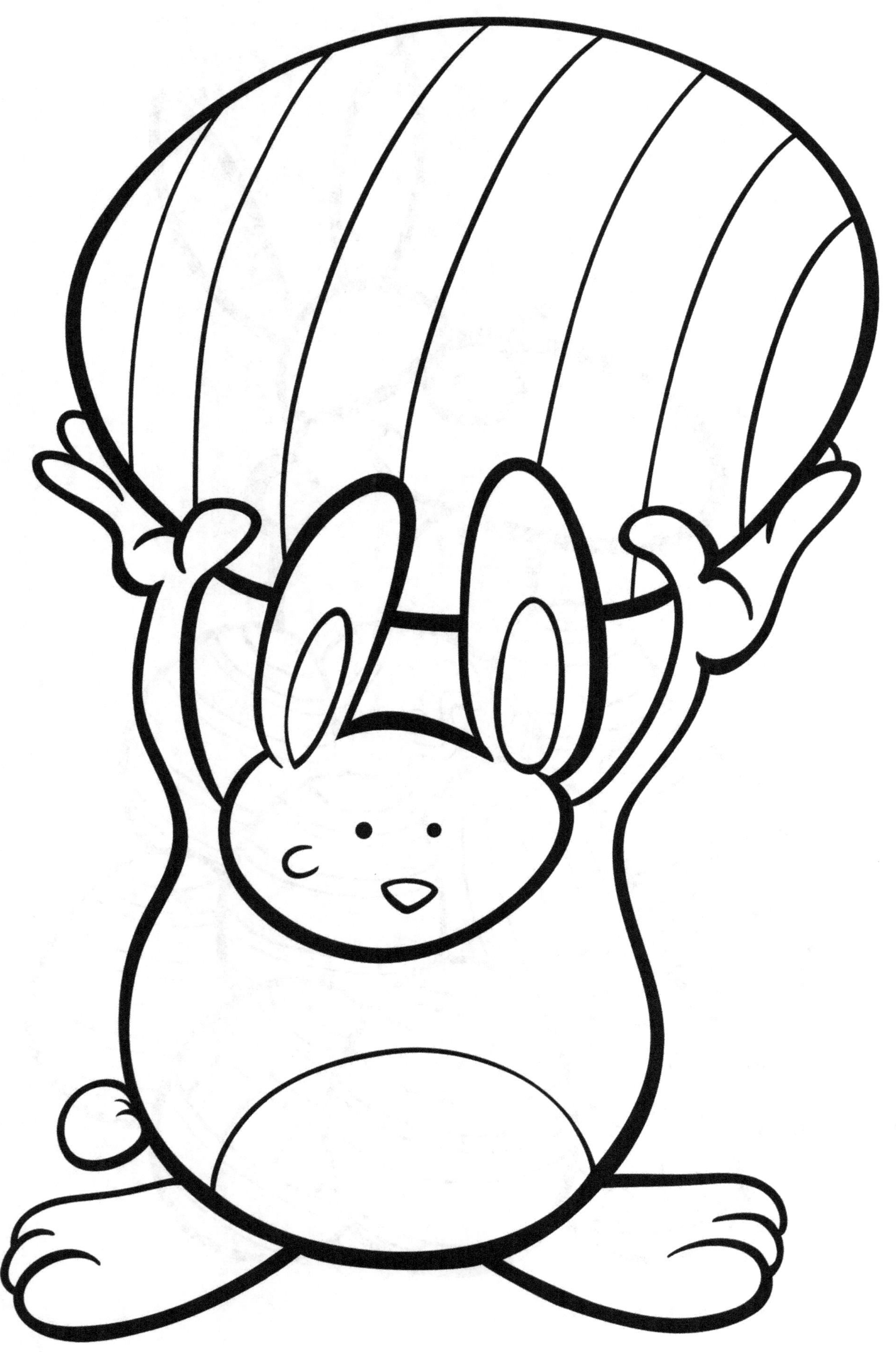

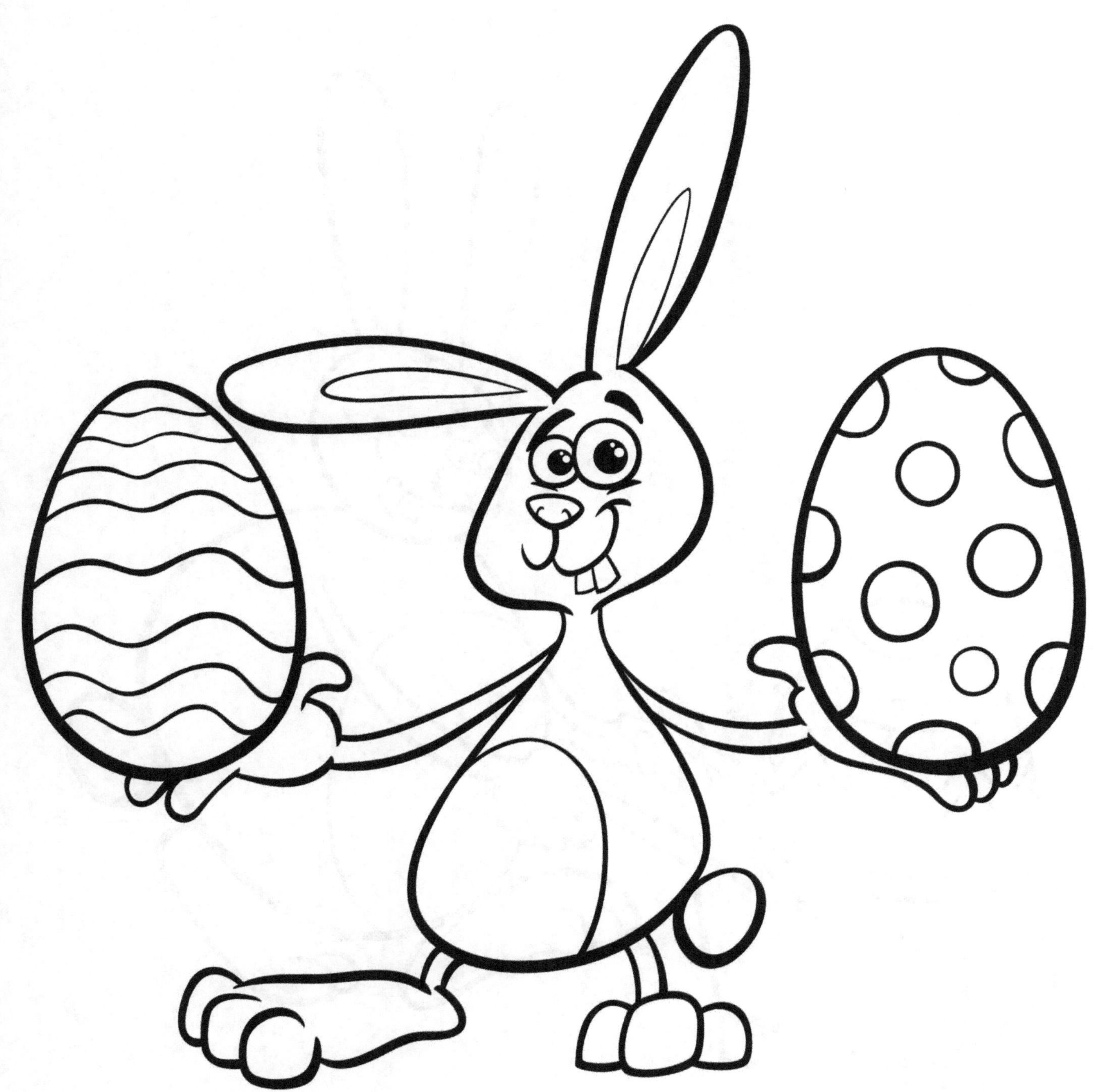

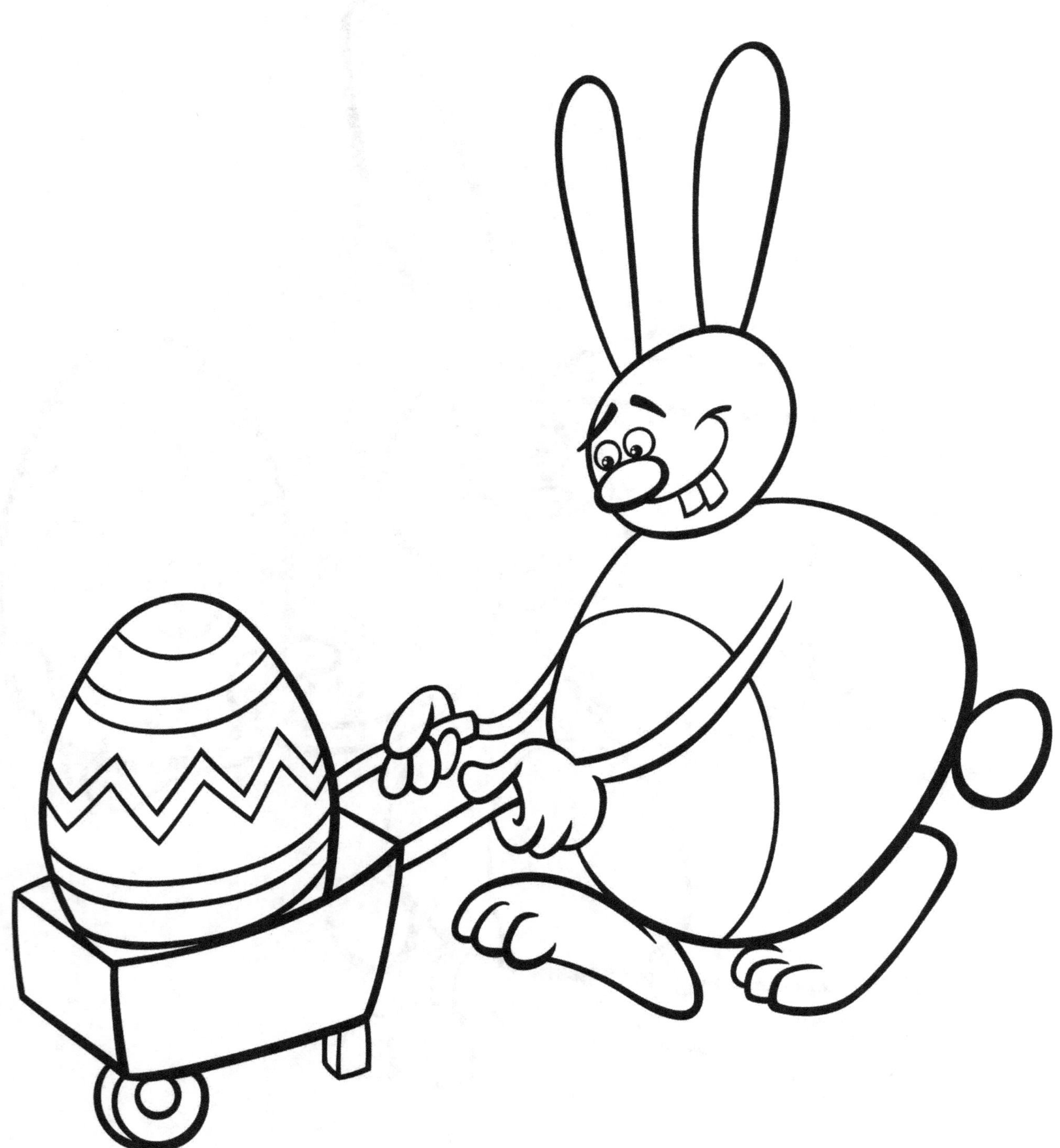

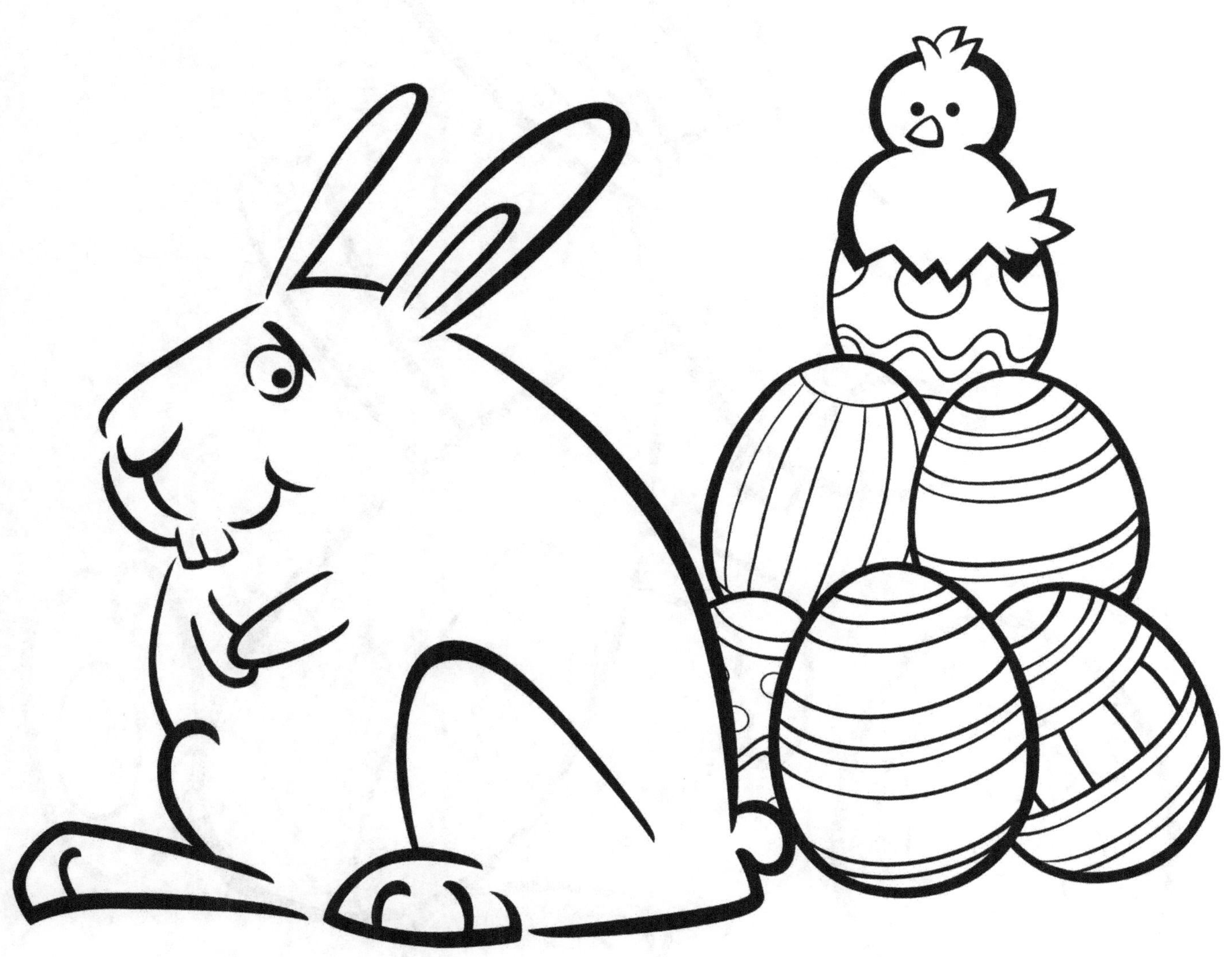

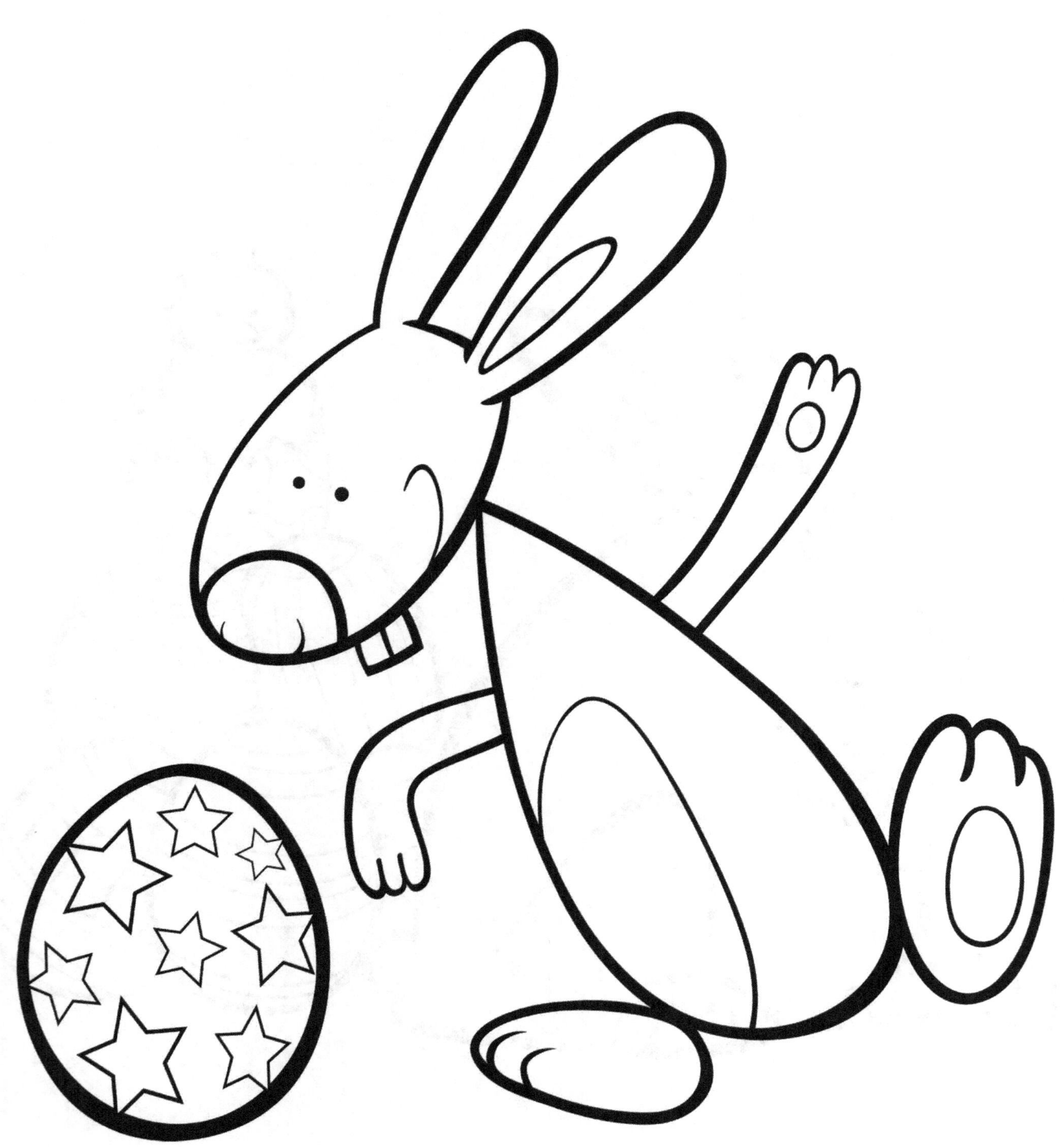

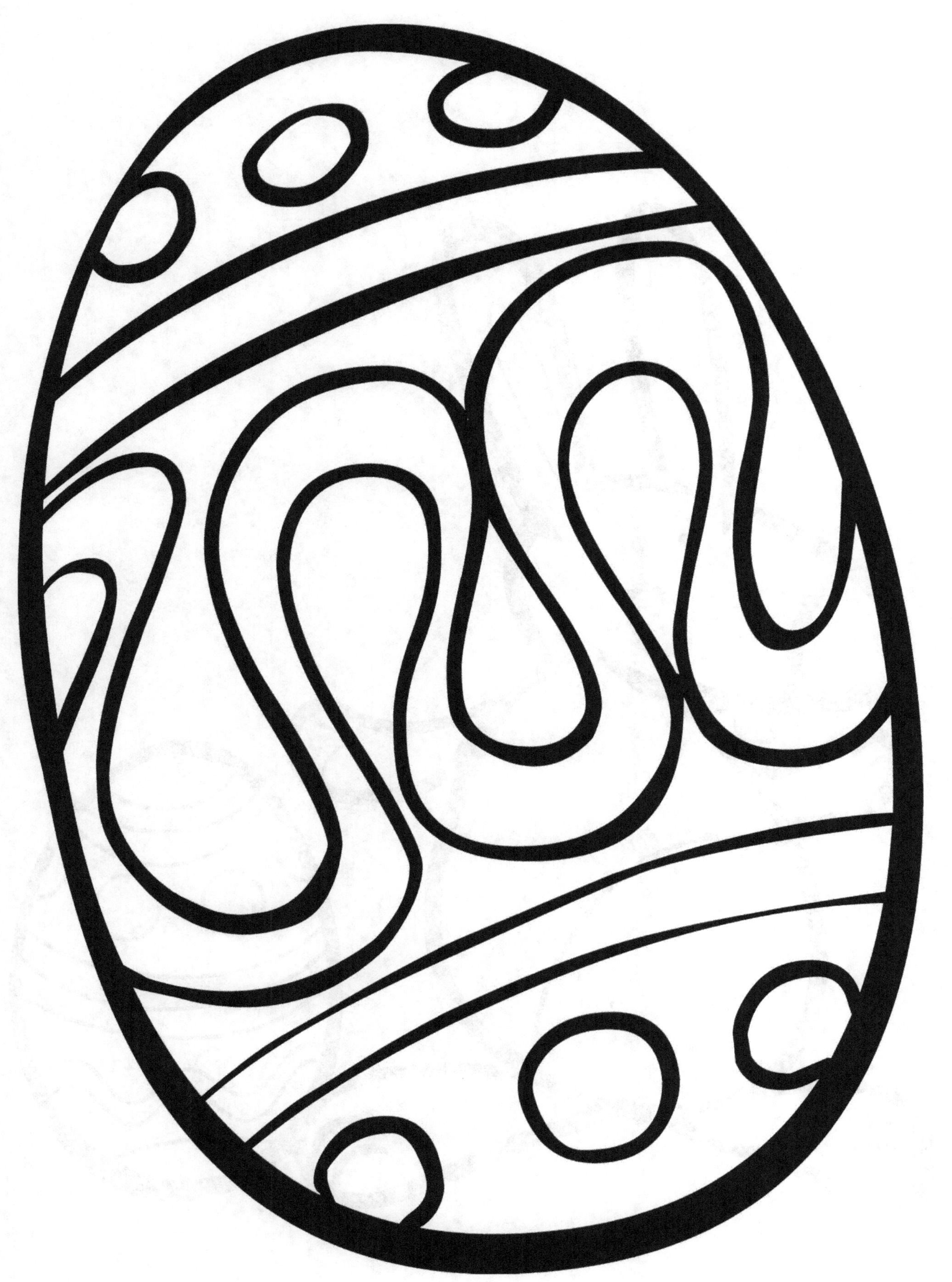

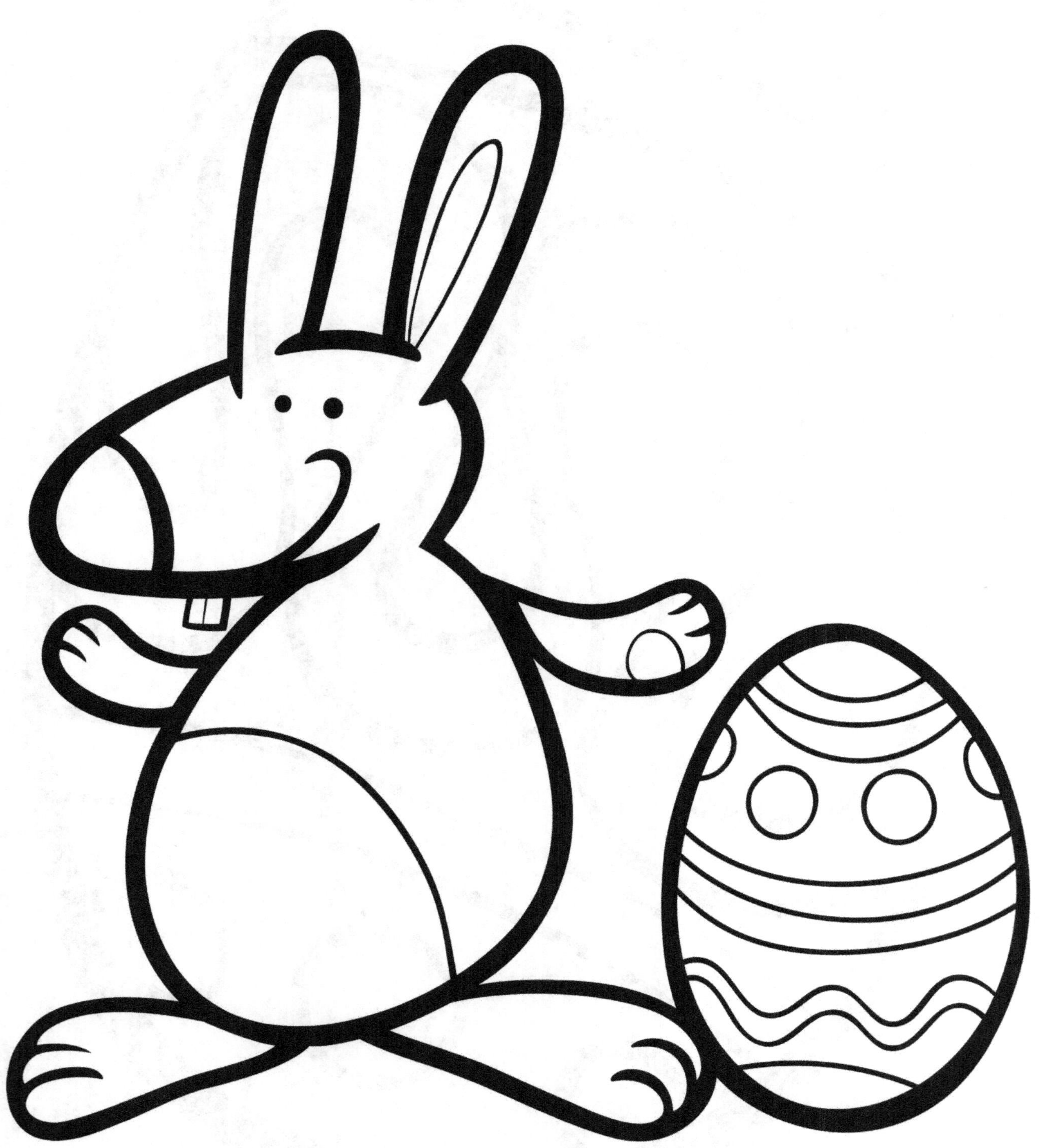

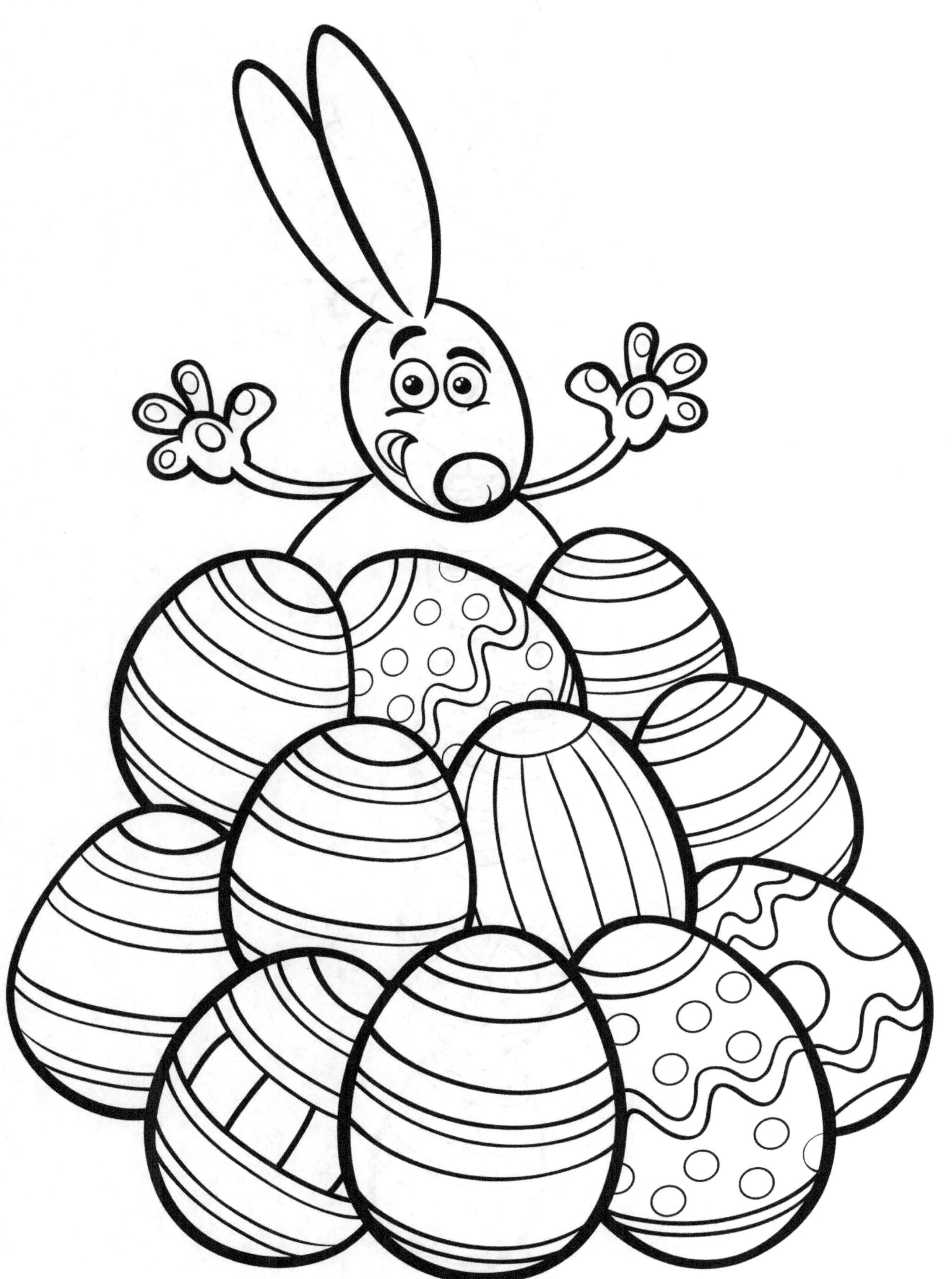

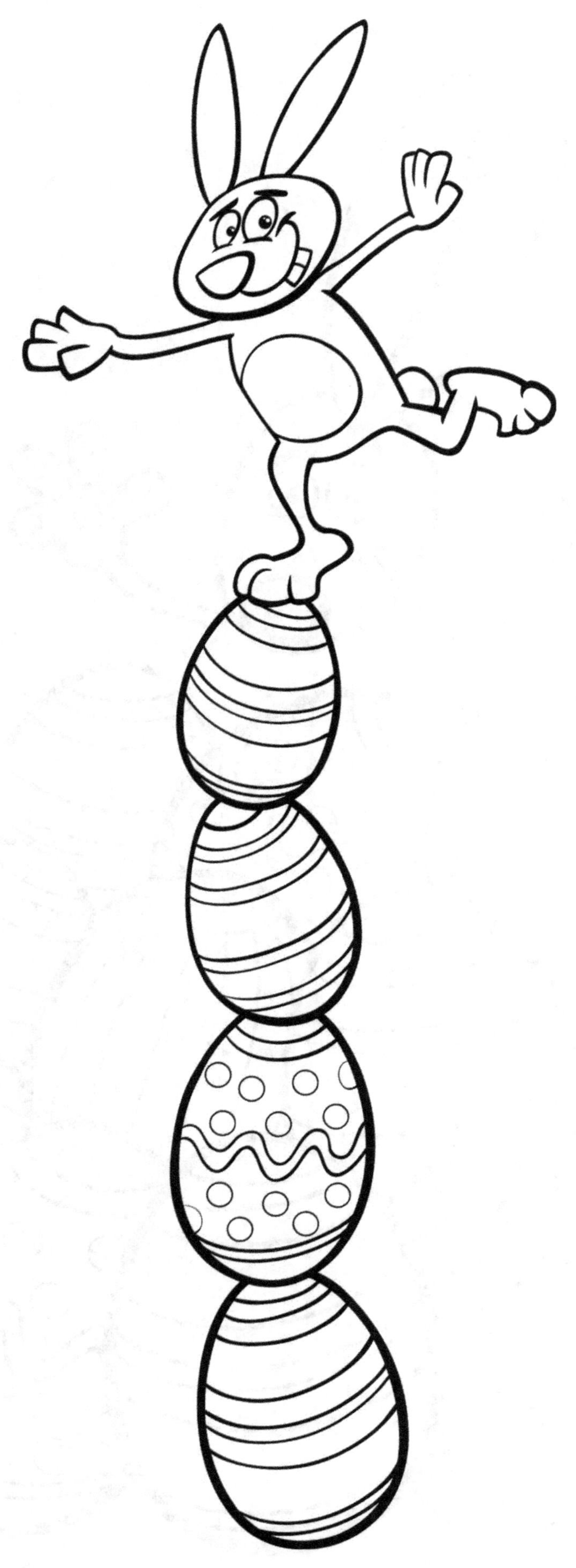

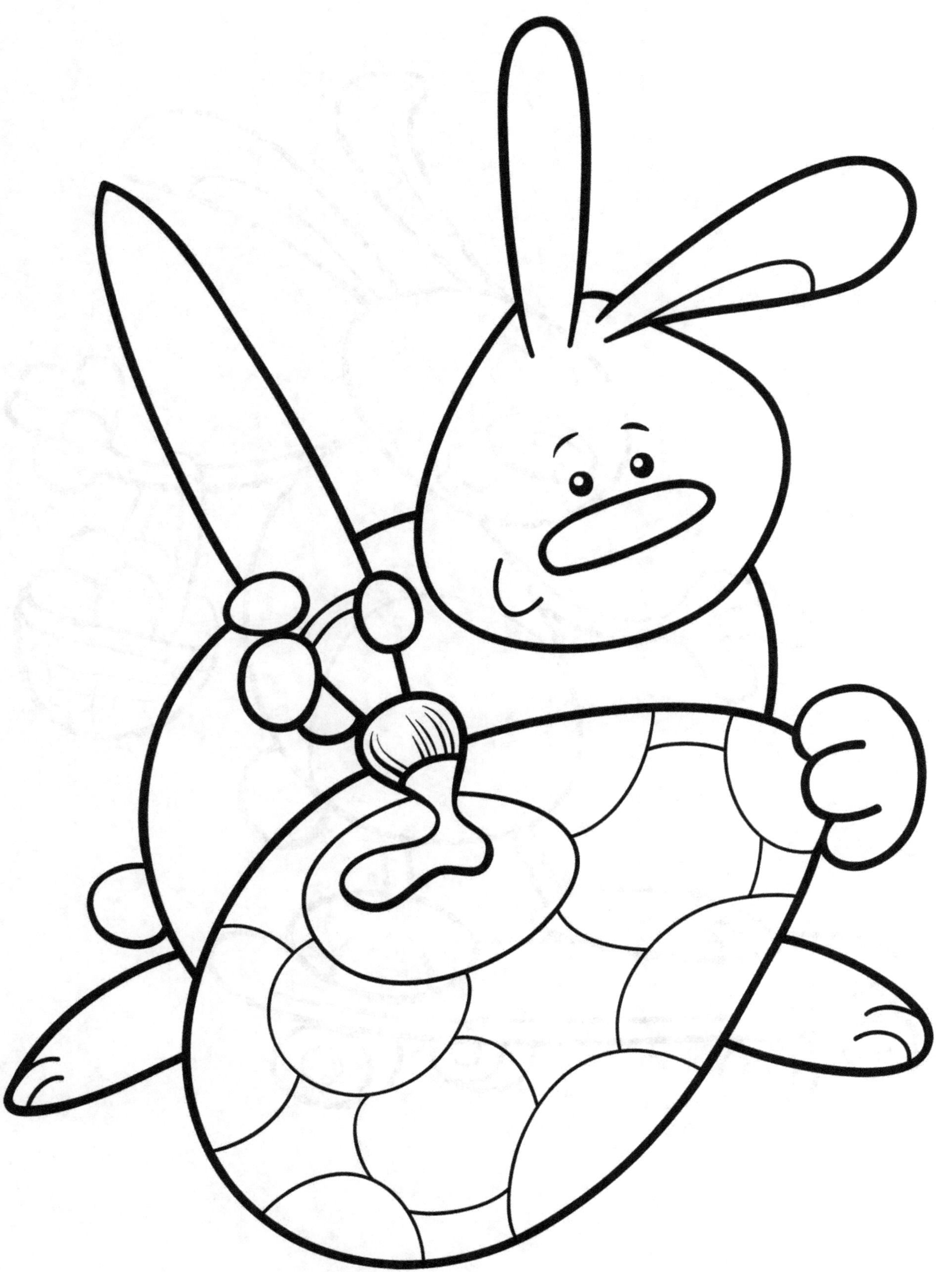

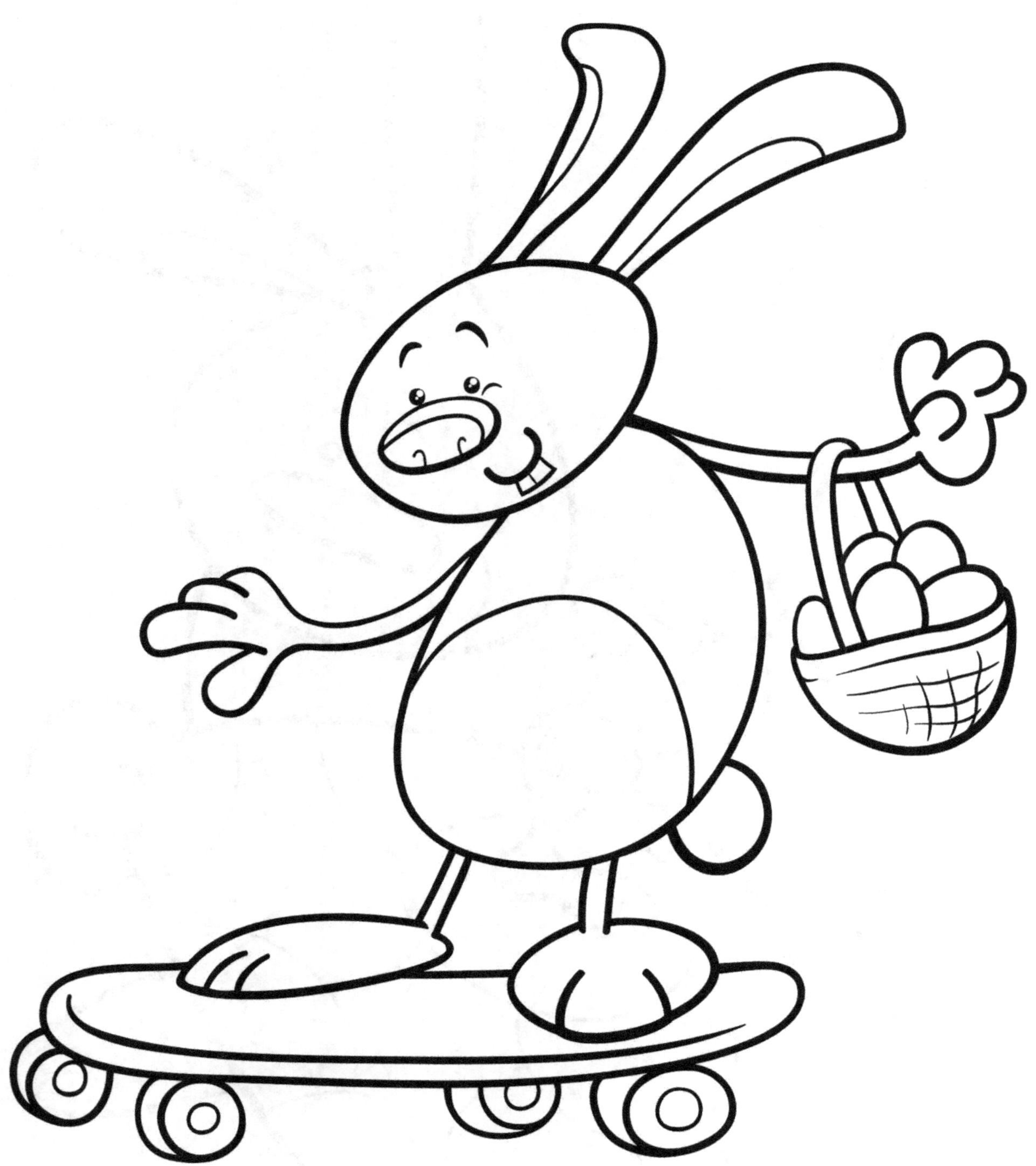

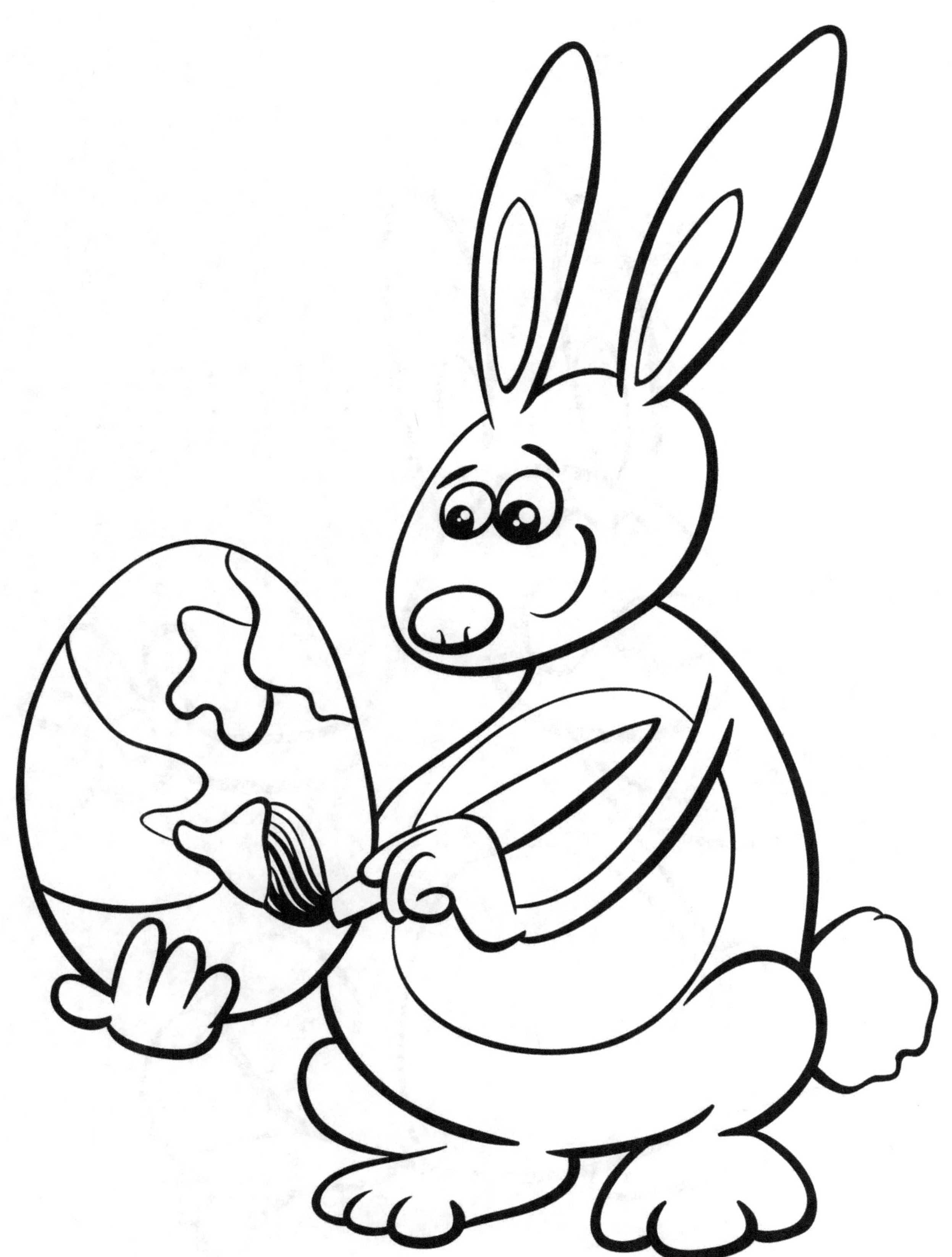

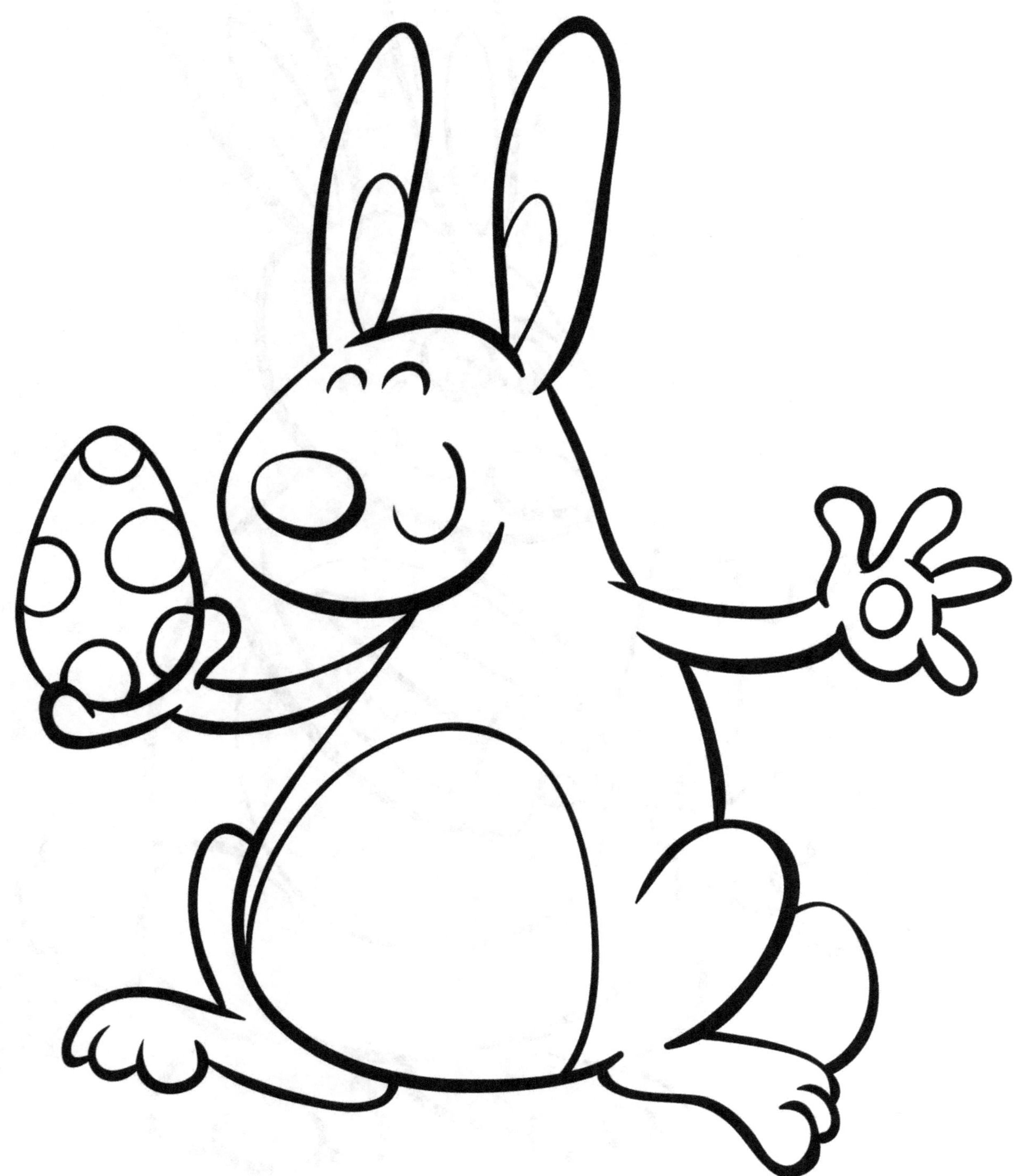